Awesome, Disgusting Careers
DISGUSTING GARBAGE JOBS
AF348832
Mary E. Bleckwehl
BLACK RABBIT BOOKS

Hi Jinx is published by Black Rabbit Books
P.O. Box 227, Mankato, Minnesota, 56002.
www.blackrabbitbooks.com
Copyright © 2023 Black Rabbit Books

Marysa Storm, editor; Michael Sellner, designer
and photo researcher

Library of Congress Cataloging-in-Publication Data
Names: Bleckwehl, Mary Evanson, author.
Title: Disgusting garbage jobs / by Mary E. Bleckwehl.
Description: Mankato, Minnesota : Black Rabbit Books, [2023] |
Series: Hi jinx. Awesome, disgusting careers | Includes bibliographical
references and index. | Audience: Ages: 8-12 | Audience: Grades: 4-6 |
Summary: "Let readers explore the awesome, disgusting garbage jobs
that keep their world running smoothly through witty, conversational
text, fun facts, and critical thinking questions that'll have them laughing
and learning"– Provided by publisher.
Identifiers: LCCN 2020030393 (print) | LCCN 2020030394 (ebook) |
ISBN 9781623106829 (hardcover) | ISBN 9781644665497 (paperback) |
ISBN 9781623106881 (ebook)
Subjects: LCSH: Refuse collectors–Juvenile literature. |
Refuse collection–Juvenile literature.
Classification: LCC HD8039.R46 B54 2022 (print) | LCC HD8039.R46
(ebook) | DDC 628.4/4023–dc23
LC record available at https://lccn.loc.gov/2020030393
LC ebook record available at https://lccn.loc.gov/2020030394

Image Credits

CONTENTS

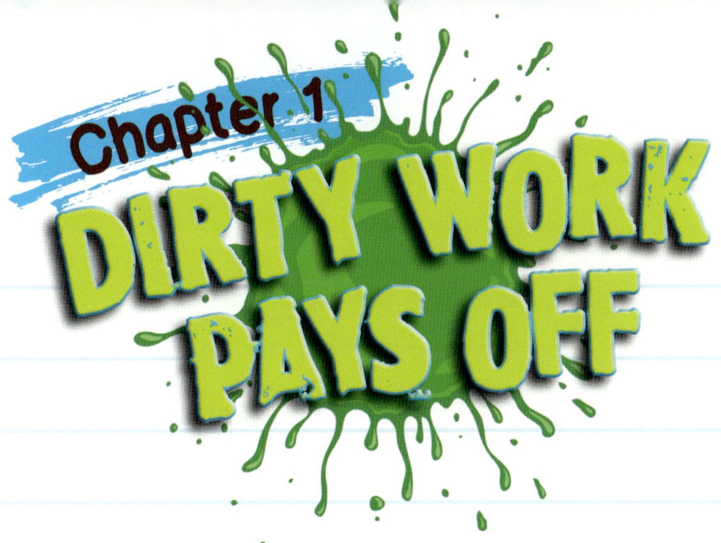

Working with garbage might not be your dream job. After all, trash is often super disgusting. But these jobs are super important. They keep the world clean and safe. They can be pretty cool too. Plug your nose, and read on. It's time to discover that garbage jobs aren't just a bunch of **rubbish**!

Park Trash Collector

The sign at the park says, "Leave No Trace." But not everyone follows the rules. That means park trash collectors need to clean up. Sometimes these workers must handle the smell of spoiled food. Other days they have to remove dead animals. Collectors do these disgusting jobs so visitors will want to return.

Visitors create about 100,000,000 pounds (45,359,237 kilograms) of trash in U.S. national parks each year.

collecting trash

removing dead animals

Event Center Custodian

Imagine seeing the Super Bowl or a concert for free! Event **custodians** get to do that. But only when duty calls. There's spilled soda and salsa in Section 12. Chunky vomit covers the stairs. Garbage cans overflow with trash. Even worse, stinky restrooms need attention. Custodians work hard before, during, and after events.

The Super Bowl makes a lot of garbage. It makes about 160,000 pounds (72,575 kg) of trash.

Garbage Collector

Whoa! That trash reeks! Thank goodness for garbage collectors. Some drive giant garbage trucks. Others hop on and off to empty bins into the trucks. But the job isn't just about driving and dumping. It's about smelling dirty diapers and chicken guts. This job is super gross. But it's also important. Garbage collectors haul away garbage that can cause **disease**. How awesome is that?

landfill
collecting gas
burning gas

Landfill Gas Plant Operator

After garbage is collected, it's taken to a landfill. There, the trash produces **methane** gas as it rots. This gas is dangerous. It's up to landfill gas plant operators to keep this danger under control. Some burn off the gas. Others use machines to turn the gas into useful energy.

A Virginia park has two trash mountains. That's right! People made the mountains by combining dirt and trash. The main mountain is 800 feet (244 meters) long.

Surgical Room Technician

After surgery, an operating room can look like a war zone. Blood and bits of bones might remain. A surgical room **technician's** job is to clean it all. They remove body parts and throw away cloths. Everything gets scrubbed. These workers also prepare the rooms. Then they help during surgeries. Their work keeps people safe and clean during it all.

In the 1800s, surgeons wore coats covered with dried blood. It was a sign of how experienced they were.

Roadkill Collector

See that dead animal on the road? It's up to roadkill collectors to remove it. Moving dead animals is easier said than done, though. Traffic flies by at dangerous speeds. The smell is disgusting. The animal may not REALLY be dead, either! To stay safe, these workers wear gloves and other protective gear. They use shovels to scoop up the **departed**. When it comes to heavier animals, they use lifts.

Crime Scene Cleaner

Sometimes, horrible things, like murders, happen. After these terrible crimes, crime scene cleaners come in. The cleaners scrape up body parts. They wash blood-spattered streets. These workers must be ready to work at any time. Protective gear, such as **biohazard** suits, keeps them safe from germs and disease. But they still need a strong stomach to do this job.

biohazard suit
Crime scene cleaners can make up to $80,000 a year.

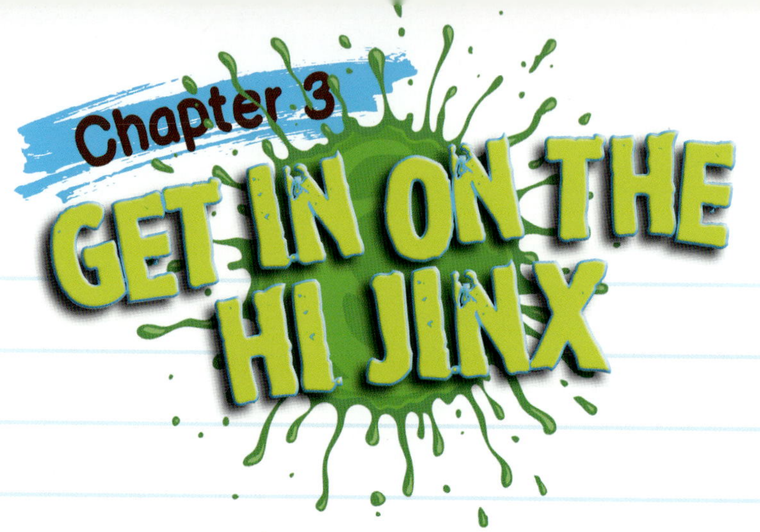

How do you land a garbage job? Most garbage jobs require a high school diploma. Then there's plenty of on-the-job training. Some jobs require technical training or a college degree. A person needs a strong stomach for any of these jobs, though. Think you're cut out for it?

Take It One Step More

1. Garbage is growing but the world isn't. Research three ways you can **reduce** garbage.

2. What is one job in this book you could never do? Why?

3. What **traits** would make a person good for the jobs in this book?

GLOSSARY

biohazard (BAHY-oh-haz-erd)—a bodily agent or condition that is a hazard to humans or the environment

custodian (kuh-STOH-dee-uhn)—a person who cleans and takes care of a building

departed (dih-PAHR-tid)—no longer living

disease (dih-ZEEZ)—an illness that affects a person, animal, or plant

methane (METH-eyn)—a colorless gas that has no smell and that can be burned for fuel

reduce (ri-DOOS)—to make something smaller in size, amount, or number

rubbish (RUHB-ish)—trash

technician (tek-NISH-uhn)—a person skilled in the detail or techniques of a subject, art, or job

trait (TREYT)—a characteristic or quality

BOOKS

Leaf, Christina. *Garbage Collectors.* Community Helpers. Minneapolis: Bellwether Media, Inc., 2019.

Nickel, Scott. *World's Grossest Jobs.* Minneapolis: Lerner Publications, 2021.

Sherman, Jill. *Garbage Collectors.* Getting the Job Done. New York: PowerKids Press, 2020.

WEBSITES

Garbage
sciencetrek.org/sciencetrek/topics/garbage/

Garbage Truck Facts for Kids
kids.kiddle.co/Garbage_truck

What Does a Garbage Collector Do?
www.careerexplorer.com/careers/garbage-collector/

INDEX